名中
人国

ONCE UPON A TIME IN CHINA

THE EMPEROR WHO BUILT THE GREAT WALL

JILLIAN LIN

Illustrations by SHI MENG

Qin Shihuang (259–210 BC),
first emperor, Qin Dynasty

Once upon a time in China...

... a boy became king when he was only thirteen years old. At the time, China was not one country as it is now. It was made up of seven kingdoms, and they were all at war with one another. The boy was the king of the smallest one, the kingdom of Qin (*Chin*).

As the kingdoms kept on fighting, the young king said, 'I'll make Qin the biggest and most powerful one of them all.'

He started to train his army and once it was ready, he began his attack on the other kingdoms. His soldiers fought for years to take over one kingdom after another.

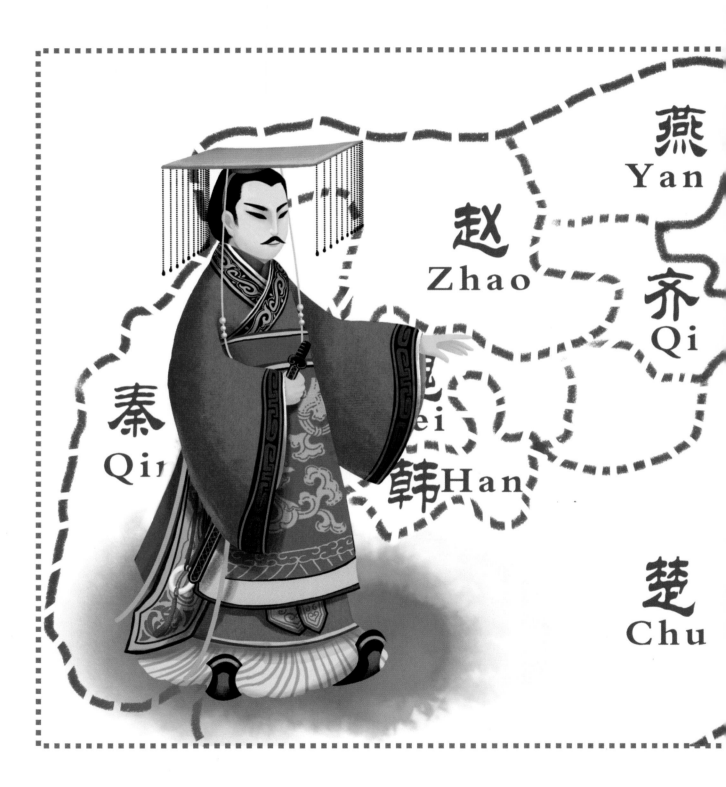

燕
Yan

赵
Zhao

齐
Qi

秦
Qin

韩Han

楚
Chu

One of the last ones to give themselves up was the kingdom of Yan. Before the army reached them, the king of Yan quickly sent a messenger to the Qin palace.

The man, called Jing, bowed deeply to the king. 'Your Highness, the king of Yan sends his best wishes. He'd also like to give you a present.'

Smiling broadly, the king of Qin said, 'Let me see it.'

Jing took a few steps closer. 'My king gives you this map of our kingdom so you can take us over peacefully, without a fight.'

Jing took out a scroll and slowly began to unroll it. The king leaned over to study the map. But at the last turn, Jing suddenly reached out and picked up a poisoned knife that was hidden inside the scroll. He pounced on the king and grabbed his sleeve. With his other hand, he pointed the knife at the king.

The king immediately jumped backwards. His sleeve tore away from Jing's hand, and the knife just missed him.

'Get that lying rat!' the king screamed to his guards.

Jing tried to run away, but it was too late. The king's guards grabbed him and dragged him away.

The king stamped on the floor in anger. 'Soldiers, attack the kingdom of Yan right now!'

At once, his army launched their attack using the map as their guide. The kingdom of Yan was taken by surprise and quickly gave up against the king's powerful army. Soon the rest of the kingdoms followed.

The king of Qin was pleased to be the leader of all seven kingdoms. He said, 'The title of king isn't enough

for the ruler of such an enormous country. From now on, I will be known as Qin Shihuang (*Chin Sheewahng*), the First Emperor of China.'

As the emperor Qin was very powerful, but he had to make sure no one could take his power away. He ordered all weapons to be melted down and turned into giant statues and bells. Only his own army was allowed to carry weapons. He also ordered for all books to be burned that were written before he became emperor.

'Anyone who breaks the law or disagrees with me,' he said, 'will be punished.'

Many people who refused to do what he had ordered were hurt or lost their lives. But even though Qin could be mean and cruel, the emperor also did a lot of good.

Before China was one country, each kingdom had their own money and system of writing. Now Qin ordered everyone in China to write the same Chinese characters and use the same round coins with a square hole in the middle.

He also built new roads and rivers to make it easier for people to buy and sell goods, and move around the country faster.

This helped bring the people from the different kingdoms together and make them feel part of the new big China.

One day, the emperor's advisers came running in with some bad news. 'Your Majesty, wild people from the north keep on attacking us. What should we do?'

Qin looked down in thought for a long while. Suddenly he leaped up.

'I have an idea.'

He pointed towards the north. 'Get as many strong men as you can get. I'm going to build a long wall to keep us safe.'

Qin got hundreds of thousands of people to work on the wall, which we now know as the Great Wall of China.

The men worked all day long in the burning heat and the bitter cold with little to eat and drink. More than one million people died building it, so the Great Wall is sometimes called 'the longest cemetery on earth'.

Over the years, Qin had become terrified of dying.

At the time, people believed that when they died, they

would begin another life called the afterlife.

That is why Qin started building a massive

underground tomb for himself. He filled it with things to

use in the afterlife including a palace, an army of clay soldiers, all kinds of valuable objects, servants, and even a zoo.

While his tomb was being built, the First Emperor ordered thousands of people to look for ways to live forever. But no one had been able to find it until an old man came to see him. He said, 'Your Majesty, I've found a magic potion that will make you live forever. It's on an island far away.'

Excited to hear this, Qin immediately went on a trip to find the magic drink. While traveling, he had a dream about strange sea creatures stopping him from getting the potion. He told his servants, 'Travel ahead to the sea and get rid of those creatures.'

His servants had no choice but to follow his orders. They returned to tell him they had been successful. Qin smiled when he heard this, believing he would soon get the potion and live forever.

Unfortunately, it was already too late. While he was on the way home, Qin fell ill and died. Clearly, not even a powerful emperor like Qin could escape death.

Nevertheless, the First Emperor had found a way to live forever. Today, more than 2,000 years later, people come from all over the world to admire the Great Wall of China and the clay warriors in the First Emperor's tomb.

Most of all, his name, 'Qin', has lived on in the word 'China'.

The End

1 ~ For each meal, servants prepared the First Emperor 100 different dishes. He could not even see and taste all the food.

2 ~ Qin was the only emperor in the history of China who did not have an empress. He had many wives, but not one who he called his special 'Number One' wife.

3 ~ Qin could be a mean and cruel emperor. He raised the tax (money people have to pay to the government). Anyone who didn't or couldn't pay, was taken prisoner and forced to work on the Great Wall as punishment.

4 ~ The Great Wall of China is the longest man-made structure in the world. It stretches through land and mountains for 13,170 miles (21,196 kilometers). That is about the distance from New York City to Punta Arenas in Chile and back.

5 ~ The Great Wall is not one long wall, but it is made up of separate parts. Many of the men who worked on the wall were prisoners and enemy soldiers.

6 ~ As the emperor, Qin did not sit on a throne, but on a raised platform. Only a few people were allowed to step on it.

7 ~ The emperor's tomb is buried deep under a hill. Inside is an army of 8,000 warriors made from terracotta, a type of clay. They look like real people, and no two are alike – every single one has a different face. Each warrior took 150 days to make.

8 ~ To keep the location of the emperor's tomb secret, thousands of workers were killed and buried after the building was finished.

9 ~ Only a tiny part of the emperor's tomb has been dug up. When you visit, all you can see are about 2,000 of the 8,000 clay soldiers. No one has ever been inside the huge underground kingdom. It is said there are mountains of gold, thousands of precious jewels set in the ceiling as stars, and flowing rivers of mercury. Mercury is a poisonous liquid metal which makes people so sick they could die. That is why the tomb has not been completely dug up.

10 ~ Qin wanted the Qin family to rule China for thousands of years. However, his son, the Second Emperor, only lasted a few years before a new emperor from the Han family took over.

1   What did the young king of Qin do to become the first emperor of China?

a)   He killed the old emperor and sat on his throne.

b)   He attacked the other six kingdoms, overtook them, and made them into one big country.

c)   He sailed to faraway lands and tell the world he was the new emperor.

2   What were some of the good changes Qin made that helped China?

a)   He made everyone write the same Chinese characters and use the same coins.

b)   He burned books that were written before he was emperor.

c)   He melted down all the weapons and turned them into statues.

Answers to the Quiz: 1. b / 2. a / 3. b / 4. c / 5. c

3   Why did the First Emperor build the Great Wall?

a)   To keep dangerous animals out of China.

b)   To keep China safe from attacks from the north.

c)   To give the people of China something to do.

4   What were some of the things found in the emperor's tomb?

a)   An army of clay warriors.

b)   A palace and a zoo.

c)   All of the above.

5   Did the First Emperor find a way to live forever?

a)   No, he died.

b)   Yes, he's still alive in his tomb.

c)   Yes and no. He died, but his name lives on in the word 'China', and what he built still exists today.

The *Once Upon A Time In China...* Series

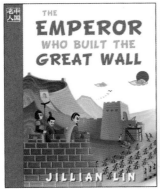
Qin Shihuang

Confucius

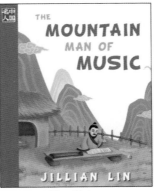
Zhu Zaiyu

Hua Tuo

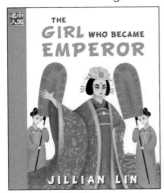
Wu Zetian

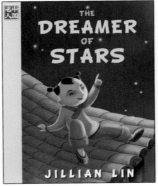
Zhang Heng

Zheng He

Koxinga

Also available as e-books. For more information, visit

www.jillianlin.com

The Emperor Who Built The Great Wall

Copyright © Jillian Lin 2016
Illustrations © Shi Meng 2016

Great Wall photo: © Anna Subbotina (depositphotos.com)
Terracotta warriors photo: © Konstantin Grishin (depositphotos.com)

Printed in Germany
by Amazon Distribution
GmbH, Leipzig